HOW TO RECOVER FROM HEARTBREAK

KEY WAYS TO GET OVER SOMEONE YOU REALLY LOVE

JEFFERY HUNTERS

Table of Contents

How Distressing Is Losing Someone You Love?

20 Steps to getting over someone you love

A Final Word on Losing Someone You Truly Loved

How do you get over someone and move on with your life when the love fades and you lose the person visitors thought was "the one"?

In a relationship cycle, letting go and moving on are the worst parts. Many negative emotions, including sadness, loneliness, depression, and many more, can be caused by it.

In the end, it might be your biggest source of unhappiness (at least for the time being).

So how do you let go of that person you've shared your life with for a very long time when the time comes? How do you convince yourself it's over and you need to move on?

We'll give you 19 suggestions in this book on how to let go of someone you love dearly and move on with your life. We offer a step-by-step procedure for reclaiming your prior, contented self and rediscovering love.

Let's first clarify how and why losing someone can be so painful before moving on to that. To learn how to let go, you first need to understand your emotions.

How Distressing Is Losing Someone You Love?

It drives you to despair.

You look for ways to win back the affection you've lost because no one was able to prepare you for it. You have the want to find that person, maintain in touch with them, and visit the locations where they might be. However, when this effort is not returned, it only makes things worse for you. It can be devastating to discover that the person you love has moved on and is spending time with someone else.

You might also make an effort to fill this void by getting involved in connections that don't actually mean anything. However, doing this can make you feel worse in the long term because you won't find the actual sense of love that you once had.

It makes you lose control over your emotions.

You know you are really upset when you start to initiate improper calls, send unwelcome messages, cry for hours, drink too much, make dramatic scenes, etc. Connected to being desperate, you feel the desire to do whatever it takes simply to get him or her back.

You are searching for a reaction of some way from this person or some form of returned attention. You might believe that if you could only catch their attention, you would have the opportunity to remind them of how wonderful the two of you were when you were together. Alternately, you may make them feel bad for you in hopes that they'll want to do something to help. You lose sight of common sense.

It causes physical agony in addition to emotional pain.

According to a 2011 study, the loss of a loved one can be a significant source of misery. Additionally, certain areas of your brain cause physical pain in response to emotional pain. Heartbreak can manifest itself in a variety of ways, including chest pain, stomachaches, appetite loss, difficulty sleeping, and excessive crying.

How to move on from someone you love dearly, someone you've never had, or someone who has abused you

Losing someone you love can hurt you physically as well as emotionally.

While some cynics hold the opinion that emotional pain can be avoided through willpower, studies have shown that the pain your heart feels after being dumped or rejected is equivalent to physical pain because your brain interprets both types of loss in the same way.

You are constrained by the past.

You repeatedly think of your relationship whenever you see his or her picture, go back to the areas you used to hang out, or watch one of their favorite movies. You simply can't let go, which is why it feels so horrible.

This is particularly true if your daily schedule, habits, or surroundings remain unchanged following your breakup. You will always be reminded of your ex-spouse, whether it be when you return home to an empty house where they used to wait for you at the end of the day or when you go to the farmer's market alone once a week.

It is often a significant cause of unhappiness.

This is among the worst types of suffering for many people. You become lost and depressed as a result. If some of your friends are particularly close to your ex, you could have expectations or ambitions for the future that are no longer realistic. You might also have to let go of some other beloved ties. You can start to doubt your life's purpose and your prospects as a result of this.

What can you do to recover from this agony and sorrow? How can you maintain your strength in the face of change? Let's examine some actions you may do to put the relationship behind you and get over your ex.

20 Steps to Overcoming a Loved One

1. If you must cry, cry a river.

You have the right to cry and experience suffering. If necessary, you can even cry. You shouldn't throw off a failed relationship too hastily. Because crying is your body's natural stress release mechanism, it instantly relieves both your mind and body.

If you don't express your emotions, it will be more difficult for you to move on. In order to prevent your emotions from building up inside and multiplying, it's critical to acknowledge them and work through them.

Permit yourself to investigate and experience the loss of what might have been.

When going through this process, make an effort to recognize your triggers and deal with them. Once you begin to recognize certain patterns in the things that trigger your emotions, you can take the necessary precautions to avoid those triggers.

After you've stopped crying, make a mental note of your emotions. You'll probably notice that your emotional state has diminished. And although while you might not immediately experience joy, you'll probably feel more at ease, less apprehensive, and prepared to move forward despite your difficulties. Hold onto this emotion and give yourself permission to cry when you need to.

2. Recognize your feelings and thoughts.

Recognizing your emotions is the best method to improve your understanding of yourself. Identify them by connecting them to a sensation, and then make an effort to comprehend it. Your emotions and thoughts are a natural part of who you are, and they serve a purpose.

It takes more than merely saying, "This is how I feel right now," to acknowledge your feelings. It involves allowing yourself to feel the feeling and then deciding what steps you will do to try to alleviate the suffering.

Your mind and body will calm down when you accept your emotions in this manner. You will benefit much from recording your ideas in a notebook so you can gain a better understanding of what took place.

3. Acknowledge that there is nothing more you can be doing about it.

You will feel helpless after a breakup or the death of a loved one, but that's acceptable. You must acknowledge that events took transpired and that there is nothing more you can do to alter them. Now, all you have to do is find out how to reclaim your joy.

You will feel worse the more you fight the end of the relationship. You won't be able to move on or heal if you keep fighting the split. But if you can learn to take the split gracefully, you'll start to feel better and develop emotional fortitude, which will ultimately bring you happiness.

How long does it take to let go of a person you still love? How quickly can you let go of someone you still love?

Gaining the ability to accept the breakup with grace can make you happier.

Accepting your situation will give you the confidence you need to build the life you want. You must identify the attitudes, ideas, and behaviors that will enable you to cope with this challenging circumstance.

4. Forgive yourself if you can't forgive the other person yet.

It can be challenging to forgive, particularly if the other person was at fault for the breakup in the first place. There may, of course, also be instances when you feel regrettable for not being able to stop bad things from happening. In that circumstance, you must first forgive yourself and acknowledge that you had no control over the situation.

It is useful to remember that we are all acting according to what we feel is correct at any given time in order to forgive ourselves for any part we may have played in the breakup or for whatever we may have done that eventually drove our partner away.

Whatever you did (or didn't do) at the time seemed to be the wisest move.

You probably wouldn't have done what you were doing if you had realized it would hurt you or your partner. Even if you were aware of the harm you were doing at the time, you probably had no idea how deeply you would later regret it. Keep in mind the lessons you took from your deeds, but let go of everything else.

5. Permit yourself to recover when you're prepared.

Before you proceed, everything must be understood. Do you feel prepared to move on? You can't let go and go on unless and until you've finally determined that you want to.

As soon as you're prepared, schedule time each day for self-care. Take up a hobby you enjoy, such as running, gardening, or meditation. This will assist you in practicing self-care that promotes recovery.

Then, encircle yourself with individuals who are encouraging of your recovery and who give you hope for the future. Always pay attention to your body's signals as well as your intuition, and follow your gut. During this time, make a conscious effort to move on with your life.

6. Acknowledge that even if this individual was significant to you, the past is now history.

It wasn't never real just because it came to an end. Even if your love for someone lasts a long time and eventually ends, it is still real and sincere. If you can't get past this one, you won't be able to finish the next tasks.

 Your past shouldn't be ignored. Your past is actually intended to be celebrated in many ways. You can reflect on what you have learnt, how you have changed, how other people have influenced you, and most importantly, who you have become now.

 Remember it, but don't cling to it. Accept the lessons it has taught you and the ways it can be of future

assistance. Keep its teachings and happy memories
near you and let them help you become a better
person.

7. Quit placing blame and calm down.

The majority of people frequently begin by blaming
another person for their own suffering. Your ex-partner
broke the law or somehow deceived you. You desire
apologies. You want them to admit to doing anything
wrong.

How Long Does It Take To Move On From Someone? | How Do You Totally Forget Someone?

Stop pointing fingers and learn to let your anger go. You will simply experience more bodily suffering as a result of this.

However, the issue with placing blame on your ex is that it renders you helpless. When they don't offer you the acknowledgement or apology you want, you're left feeling angry and without any sense of closure, which hurts you more than it does them.

You must permit yourself to experience these emotions because they are valid. But after that, you must continue. It takes a lot of energy to hold onto hatred and resentment. They add to the discomfort you're experiencing physically. Your health will suffer if you continue to experience these unfavorable feelings.

8. Discard anything that makes you think about that individual.

Items will only get worse if you keep running into things that make you think of your ex and the previous relationship you had. You'll experience regret, melancholy, and nostalgia as a result. Put them in a box and store them somewhere you can't easily reach them if you can't toss them away.

Anything sentimental or important that belongs to your ex should be returned. Don't dispose of items like their childhood teddy bear or winter overcoat, for instance, if they are at your home. Return them with respect, just as you would want they would do for you.

Why not maintain a more accurate record of your shifting emotions? See these fantastic mood-tracking apps.

9. End all correspondence with this person.

Don't schedule a meeting with them. Do not message that person (if he or she texts you first, do not reply).

Avoid calling them. You won't be able to move on if you keep the channels of communication open because doing so amounts to leaving the door open to the relationship.

Keep your talks brief and to the point if you must react to your ex's message due to significant and urgent issues. Be the first to stop speaking or reacting if the topic of discussion veers off-topic.

Last but not least, block or unfriend them on your social networking platforms. Avoid giving in to the need to check out their profile to see what they're up to and refrain from posting anything on social media with the intention of making your ex envious. Simply avoid interaction by blocking them.

get over someone, how to do it quickly, and how to do it with a person you like

10. Take part in outdoor activities and physical activity.

According to some experts, keeping yourself occupied with other activities is one of the greatest ways to move on and get over breaking up with someone you love. Exercise and other comparable activities are advised because they promote the production of hormones that make you feel cheerful. Exercise has a ton of other health advantages that can improve your general well-being and may even help you get a hot revenge body.

Try boxing to let your anger out or enroll in an HIIT fitness class to keep your mind active. Yoga is a great way to help you reestablish your connection to who you are and find your core.

11. Physically tidy up the mess!

Prepare yourself and lift yourself up. You cannot progress if you are surrounded by chaos. According to research, living in an organized environment promotes living in an organized way.

Make your own "trash," "donation," and "keep" piles as you sift through your belongings and sort your ex's stuff into categories for disposal or return. By doing this, you'll feel revived and refreshed as you make room in your home for fresh items.

12. Go gently and take things one day at a time.

Keep in mind that there is no pressing need, and you should give yourself the space to grieve. The entire process cannot be hurried. Expecting to recover from a broken heart overnight is unrealistic. As long as everything is done correctly, it doesn't matter how long the procedure takes.

How to get over a person quickly, how to get over a person you like, or how to get over a person who abused you

There is no short way to progress. Don't rush the whole thing. Take things carefully and in baby steps.

Of course, this does not imply that you should stay in bed and wallow in your misery forever because you are thinking about your ex. However, take things one step at a time, and you'll start to see results.

13. Exercise patience and never lose faith in yourself.

Once more, grieving the loss of a loved one takes time. Before you can completely let go and go on, it can take weeks, months, or even years. But remain certain that you will complete the procedure, whatever how difficult and drawn-out it may be. Keep in mind that you were fine before you met your ex, and you will continue to be well as your life moves forward without them.

Even though it might not seem like it, you are moving closer to moving past your ex. Be kind to yourself and keep believing you will overcome this. Relationships may become more strained if you begin to lose hope in yourself and in others. Having faith in oneself.

[Want your level of happiness to rise. By encouraging a series of happy exercises, these top happiness apps will assist you in monitoring, tracking, and really increasing your life happiness.]

14. Ignore the past and pay attention to the present.

Quit torturing yourself with hypothetical scenarios and "if only" arguments. Recognize the beauty around you and be grateful for what life still has to give. By embracing the present moment without passing judgment and avoiding dwelling on the past or the future, you can practice mindfulness.

You can develop thankfulness for the positive aspects of your life by keeping your attention in the present. It might assist you in realizing that while this relationship was a component of who you are, it did not define you. It might be your amazing friends, family, job, hobbies, pets, or other possessions that genuinely define who you are.

15. Be excited about what the future may hold.

Your relationship might have ended because a better, more fulfilling one is waiting for you in the future, but everything happens for a reason. The breakup can turn out to be advantageous. You are being prepared for the future through life. There are countless options for your future.

Make a plan for your future during this time that you have to yourself. Regain control of your life by being self-centered in your decisions about how and with whom to spend your time. You can use this to mold a future that is full of exciting new possibilities.

16. Take a lesson from this encounter.

Make sure you take something away from this experience because it was a significant one in your life. You'll be better prepared to handle things if you experience it again in the future (let's hope not!).

Make a note of the coping mechanisms that are effective for you and give you a sense of empowerment. Find the things in your life that truly make you happy or enable you to escape any negativity in your immediate environment. If you ever find yourself in a scenario like this again, keep these suggestions in mind.

17. Be willing to consider potential new partnerships.

After a severe heartbreak, many people choose to shut their doors. Don't act in such manner. Though it's difficult, you must attempt to regain your faith and find love.

How long does it take to get over a person you still care about? How do you get over a person who has abused you?

Keep the possibility of a new connection open. You must make an effort even if it could be difficult to trust and fall in love again.

Keep yourself open to the prospect of moving on with someone else even though you may not want to immediately enter a new relationship. Until you start to feel contented with someone else, you might not recognize that you are truly over your ex.

18. Discover solace in the company of your loved ones.

Your spouse might have left you, but your real family and friends never will. Going home is the only way to feel safe after all other options have failed. Spend time with those who have known you the longest to simplify things once more.

These folks will not only be able to soothe you but will also serve as a reminder of your identity and origins. They'll assist you get back on track and start over.

19. Spend some time loving yourself

Never undervalue the importance of loving yourself.

I'm not referring to narcissistic levels of self-love. But before others can love us back, we must first learn to love ourselves. The malaise of a failed relationship can be lifted with a little self-pampering, and it can also offer you the mental clarity you need to find yourself a new and better relationship amid the ashes of your previous one.

20. Look for expert assistance—visit a therapist or sign up for a support group.

This is a possibility for people who are genuinely struggling to move on from a failed relationship or a lost love. Your current emotions are normal; following a breakup, people commonly experience sadness and loneliness. Therefore, there is no reason to be embarrassed or reluctant about obtaining expert assistance.

Therapists or other individuals living through comparable circumstances might support you by empathizing with your sentiments and validating your feelings. You can improve yourself only by telling your experience and allowing yourself to relate to others.

A Final Word on Losing Someone You Truly Loved

It takes time to move on from a painful breakup and get over a significant other in your life. It is not now and never will be simple.

But you must continue to struggle. You have to maintain your composure and strive to get better, despite how challenging or unpleasant it may be.

We've discussed how losing someone may make your life unpleasant and sad in this piece. But we've also discussed how it's possible to let the past go and have a better life.

Despite all of your difficulties, you will eventually become the happier person you deserve to be. You simply need to figure out how and be prepared.

We sincerely hope that the advice we provided would enable you to let go of the person you genuinely love.

If you want to develop your ability to invest in yourself

and learn to appreciate yourself more.

Follow your gut and do what seems right to you. Even

after the most agonizing heartbreak, celebrate life.